The Holy Week

FOR LATTER-DAY SAINT FAMILIES

2016

Wendell W. Roskom

*To Monika Rosborough-Bowman,
a mother who knows. She has inspired me to find
deeper religious meaning in every holiday.*

The Holy Week

FOR LATTER-DAY SAINT FAMILIES

A Guide for Celebrating Easter

WENDEE WILCOX ROSBOROUGH

foreword by Brad Wilcox

DESERET
BOOK

SALT LAKE CITY, UTAH

Image credits:
Wendee Wilcox Rosborough, 4 top, 5, 7, 14, 15, 21, 22, 28, 29, 30 top, 36, 37, 44, 46, 47, 53, 54, 55, 61, 69, 70.
smallseedblog, 4 bottom, 23, 63.
iStock, 6, 12, 13, 38, 39, 45, 52, 64, 68.
Shutterstock, 30 bottom, 60.
Walter Rane, viii.
Hope Gallery, 8, 32.
Bridgeman Art Library, 16, 24.
J. Kirk Richards, 40.
Robert Barrett, 48.
Brigham Young University Museum of Art, 56 (Minerva Teichert (1888–1976), *Touch Me Not*, 1937, oil on canvas,
    76½ x 59¾ inches).

© 2016 Wendee Wilcox Rosborough

Library of Congress Cataloging-in-Publication Data

Rosborough, Wendee Wilcox, author.
    The Holy Week for Latter-day Saint families : a guide for celebrating Easter / Wendee Wilcox Rosborough ; foreword by Brad Wilcox.
        pages cm
    Includes bibliographical references.
    ISBN 978-1-62972-148-4 (paperbound)
    1. Holy Week. 2. The Church of Jesus Christ of Latter-day Saints—Customs and practices. I. Title.
    BV90.R67 2016
    242'.35—dc23   2015034647

Printed in China
RR Donnelley, Shenzhen, China

10 9 8 7 6 5 4 3 2 1

Contents

Foreword
BRAD WILCOX

Our family has always enjoyed Easter. It meant egg coloring, Easter baskets, egg hunts, and candy. Sometimes the girls got new dresses; sometimes we took a family picture. At church, we usually sang "He Is Risen!" (*Hymns,* 199) and heard talks and testimonies about the Resurrection of Christ. These are all important traditions and moments of worship. However, it was only when living abroad that we realized there were additional aspects of the Easter holiday that could add depth to our celebration and help us better remember the Savior. In Chile, Christians celebrated *la Semana Santa,* or the Holy Week. When Wendee married an Italian, we admired how seriously he and his family took *Pasqua* or *Settimana Santa* each year. Christians worldwide make efforts to remember the last week of Jesus' life as well as His glorious Resurrection. Our family determined to commemorate this special season with increased devotion. I am proud of my oldest daughter, Wendee, for creating this much-needed book— an invitation to families everywhere to join us in celebrating Easter all week long.

The actual chronology of Jesus' final week in mortality is a little hard to piece together, since the gospels differ in their accounts. Rather than worrying about the exact order of multiple events each day, Wendee has chosen to focus on general themes and provided multiple activities from which families may choose in order to commemorate one aspect of the Holy Week. This smorgasbord of ideas will make the book a beloved resource and keep celebrations fresh from year to year. Although this book was created with children in mind, many of the activities can involve the entire family. Teenagers will learn a great deal as they prepare and lead activities for younger siblings.

Elder Jeffery R. Holland wrote, "The inner state . . . gives meaning to the outer gesture" (*For Times of Trouble* [Salt Lake City: Deseret Book, 2012], 58). I am confident that this book will inspire your family to remember sacred events of long ago and more fully realize their significance in our lives today.

Palm Sunday
THE TRIUMPHAL ENTRY

John 12:12–13

On the next day much people that were come to the feast, when they heard that Jesus was coming to Jerusalem, took branches of palm trees, and went forth to meet him, and cried, Hosanna: Blessed is the King of Israel that cometh in the name of the Lord.

See also Mathew 21:1–11; Luke 19:28–38.

Art Appreciation

Triumphal Entry, **by Walter Rane.** American artist and Church member Walter Rane has been fascinated with the power of art since childhood. He has found painting to be a meaningful way to express his gratitude for and testimony of the Savior.

Memory Scripture

"Hosanna! Blessed be the name of the Most High God! And they did fall down at the feet of Jesus, and did worship him" (3 Nephi 11:17).

Watch the Story Come to Life

"The Lord's Triumphal Entry into Jerusalem" video

https://www.lds.org/media-library/video
/2011-10-017-the-lords-triumphal-entry
-into-jerusalem?lang=eng

Learn through Song

"Hosanna," *Children's Songbook*, 66

"Easter Hosanna," *Children's Songbook*, 68

HOW DOES PALM SUNDAY REMIND US OF JESUS?

On the Sunday before Easter, Christians throughout the world wave branches in memory of Jesus entering the city of Jerusalem. On that triumphant day, He humbly rode a donkey through the streets. People were so happy to see Him that they waved palm branches and shouted, "Hosanna!" The word *hosanna* comes from Hebrew and means "save now, we pray."

When Latter-day Saint temples are dedicated, members wave white handkerchiefs above their heads and shout, "Hosanna!" (see D&C 19:37, 36:3), just like Christ's disciples in Jerusalem did with palm branches. When the first Mormon pioneers entered the Salt Lake Valley, they also waved handkerchiefs and shouted, "Hosanna!" These moments remind us not only of how people welcomed the Savior to the temple at Jerusalem, but also how we must welcome Jesus into our lives and hearts.

Saying "Hosanna" shows we understand that Jesus is the only one who could have performed the Atonement, the only one with power to help us return to our Father in Heaven and live with loved ones eternally. It shows we realize how much we need and depend on Him.

Shouting "Hosanna" also shows how happy we are to know Jesus fulfilled Heavenly Father's plan. Before we came to earth we knew that He would be our Savior, so we shouted for joy (see Job 38:7). In the Book of Mormon, the people who met Jesus also shouted for joy (see 3 Nephi 4:32). When Jesus comes again, we will shout for joy as well (see 1 Thessalonians 4:16). When we wave branches or handkerchiefs and shout "Hosanna," we can remember Jesus and be happy that He came and will come again.

Here are some ideas to help you celebrate and learn. Choose what works best for your family!

Easter Story Wreath

Begin an Easter story wreath that you can add to throughout the week. Have family members draw various images that represent the theme for each day (a palm branch or donkey for Sunday, a temple for Monday, and so on). Cut out the drawings and arrange them in a circle. Staple, tape, or glue a new drawing onto the wreath each day, and display your Easter wreath somewhere the whole family can see.

Easter Tree

You can create an Easter centerpiece for your table using any type of branch. It could be artificial or real. Cut out egg shapes from colored paper or cardstock, punch a hole at the top of each one, and then tie a loop of ribbon or string through each hole so the eggs can hang like ornaments. Have family members write or draw blessings made possible because of the Atonement on the paper eggs, and hang the eggs on the branch. Throughout the week, gather the family together and invite someone

to choose an ornament from the "tree" and read or describe the blessing on it. Consider using that blessing as a discussion topic during a meal or family time.

Blessing Branch

Cut out strips of green paper, and invite family members to think of blessings they have received from God and write them on the strips. Glue or tape the strips to a larger piece of construction paper or poster board in the shape

of a palm branch (or to a real branch!) and display it somewhere in your home to show gratitude for your blessings.

Palm Leaf Napkin Folding

Help children fold cloth or paper napkins into palm leaves. These can make your dinner special. Take a square napkin and fold it in half. With the folded edge at the top, accordion fold across the entire napkin, folding back and forth in alternating directions. Pinch together the bottom of the folded-up napkin and place it in a glass, folding it over once to make a sturdy base (see image). Then fan out the top of the napkin to create the leaf.

Reenactment

Use sidewalk chalk to create a Jerusalem street path on your driveway. Have an older child or parent pretend to be the donkey on all fours, and have a younger child ride on the "donkey's" back while the rest of the family waves handkerchiefs or palm branches cut out of construction paper. Cheer "Hosanna!" Make sure to keep a spirit of reverence as you reenact the triumphal entry of the Savior.

Living Plant

People waved palm branches to welcome and honor Jesus, but eventually those branches died. Jesus came to Jerusalem to overcome death through the Atonement, so planting a seed that will grow into a living plant is a wonderful way to honor Him. You can plant seeds in cups of soil. Lentils grow extremely fast, so they're a good choice for letting children see growth quickly. Soak the lentils in water for a few hours to soften beforehand, and then plant a small handful in a paper cup of soil. Water daily and place near a window for sunshine. When children become excited seeing their plants grow, you can take the opportunity to emphasize that the living plant reminds us of the living Christ.

Cleansing Monday

SANCTIFYING THE TEMPLE

Matthew 21:12–15

And Jesus went into the temple of God, and cast out all them that sold and bought in the temple, and overthrew the tables of the moneychangers, and the seats of them that sold doves, and said unto them, It is written, My house shall be called the house of prayer; but ye have made it a den of thieves. And the blind and the lame came to him in the temple; and he healed them. And when the chief priests and scribes saw the wonderful things that he did, and the children crying in the temple, and saying, Hosanna to the Son of David; they were sore displeased.

See also Mark 11:15–18; Luke 19:45–48.

Art Appreciation

Christ Cleansing the Temple, **by Carl Bloch.** Carl Heinrich Bloch was born in Copenhagen Denmark in 1834—just four years after the Church was organized in New York. Bloch was asked to illustrate the life of Christ for the king's prayer chamber in Frederiksborg Castle, and this painting was one of twenty-three scenes created. His paintings show he had a deep understanding of Jesus Christ's role as our Savior.

Memory Scripture

"Know ye not that your body is the temple of the Holy Ghost which is in you?" (1 Corinthians 6:19).

Watch the Story Come to Life

"Jesus Cleanses the Temple" video

https://www.lds.org
/media-library/video
/2011-10-039-jesus
-cleanses-the-temple
?lang=eng

"Standing in Holy Places" video

https://www.lds.org
/youth/video
/standing-in-holy
-places?lang=eng

Learn through Song

"This Is God's House," *Children's Songbook*, 30

"The Lord Gave Me a Temple," *Children's Songbook*, 153

HOW DOES CLEANSING THE TEMPLE REMIND US OF JESUS?

When Jesus went to the temple in the last week of His mortal ministry, He was discouraged to see people who were there for the wrong reasons. In those days, people had to pay tithing with special coins made just for that purpose. That meant they had to change their regular money into tithing money. A lot of greedy men set up shops in the temple and charged too much for changing money so they could get richer. Other people sold animals for sacrifice, but they also charged more than they should have. Jesus cast them out to keep the temple a holy place.

Earlier Jesus had taught, "The foxes have holes, and the birds of the air have nests; but the Son of man hath not where to lay his head" (Matthew 8:20). A hole is a fox's house, and a nest is a bird's house. President Ezra Taft Benson said that the temple "had been desecrated. . . . The Son of Man had no place to lay his head because there was no dedicated, acceptable house of the Lord" ("Remarks," *Ensign,* May 1980, 94).

Thanks to the restoration of the gospel, the Lord *does* have a place to call home. He has many houses all across the world—temples. The temple is a place where we feel peace and receive personal revelation. In the temple, we learn important lessons about who we are and God's plan for us. We receive sacred ordinances for ourselves and then offer the same opportunity to people who have passed away. The temple is the only place where families can be bound and united—sealed—together forever.

Just as the temple needed to be cleansed for the Spirit to dwell within it, we need to invite Jesus to cleanse and sanctify us so we can be worthy of the Spirit. We can prepare ourselves by choosing to obey the commandments and to repent—change and be better—when we fail. We can make covenants in baptism and renew those covenants each week as we attend church and partake of the sacrament. When we see a temple and keep ourselves worthy to go there, we can remember Jesus and honor sacred covenants.

Here are some ideas to help you celebrate and learn. Choose what works best for your family!

Temple Testimonies

Visit the nearest temple grounds or show one another favorite pictures of the temple, and share your testimonies of the importance of temples. Encourage children to share feelings or memories relating to temples. A good way to introduce this activity is to share a quote from a Church leader, such as the following thought from Elder Robert E. Wells: "Our feelings about the temple are the truest indicators of our deepest feelings about Christ" (*Hasten My Work* [Salt Lake City: Bookcraft, 1996], 85).

Ten-Minute Cleanup

Remind children that the Spirit cannot dwell in unholy places (see D&C 97:17). Our homes need to stay clean and pure like the temple. The Bible Dictionary teaches that "only the home can compare with the temple in sacredness." Write simple chores on slips of paper and put them in a bowl. Have each family member choose a task out of the bowl, and then set a timer for ten minutes. See if everyone can finish his or her assigned chore within the time allotted.

Gratitude Letters

After Jesus cleansed the temple, He healed people (see Matthew 21:14). Temples are places where we are anointed and blessed. As a family, read John 12:1–8, which tells about when Mary anointed Jesus at Bethany. Take turns giving compliments and letting family members know how much you value them. Consider writing gratitude letters, cards, or emails to relatives who live far away or friends in your ward as a form of "blessing" others.

Homemade Play Dough

2 cups water

½ cup salt

1½ tablespoons alum powder (found in the spice aisle of grocery store)

3 tablespoons baby oil

food coloring (any color)

3½–4 cups flour

Combine water and salt in a medium-sized bowl and microwave for 3½ minutes.

Add alum powder, baby oil, food coloring, and 3½ cups of flour and mix.

Turn dough out onto a lightly floured surface and knead thoroughly, adding enough flour to reach desired consistency.

Allow dough to cool before storing in a resealable bag to preserve for future use.

Sculpt It

Make homemade play dough and sculpt temples or temple-related words from the bank below. Consider dividing into teams and making a game of it—one member of each team tries to sculpt the same word while his or her teammates try to guess what is being sculpted. The first team to correctly guess the word gets a point!

Moroni	wedding bouquet	sunstone
person praying	temple recommend	chandelier
spire	family	temple
Solomon's Temple	house	moon
wedding dress	window	beehive
baptismal font	bishop	oxen
scriptures	door	

Parable Tuesday
TEACHING THE DISCIPLES

Matthew 13:10–13, 16

And the disciples came, and said unto him, Why speakest thou unto them in parables? He answered and said unto them, Because it is given unto you to know the mysteries of the kingdom of heaven, but to them it is not given. For whosoever hath, to him shall be given, and he shall have more abundance: but whosoever hath not, from him shall be taken away even that he hath. Therefore speak I to them in parables: because they seeing see not; and hearing they hear not, neither do they understand. But blessed are your eyes, for they see: and your ears, for they hear.

Art Appreciation

The Return of the Prodigal Son, **by Rembrandt.** Rembrandt Harmenszoon van Rijn, commonly known as Rembrandt, was a Dutch artist who was moved by the parable of the prodigal son. He created many drawings, etchings, and paintings about that parable throughout his life. This painting of the return of the prodigal son is considered one of Rembrandt's finest works and was completed shortly before his death in 1669.

Memory Scripture

"Then Simon Peter answered him, Lord, to whom shall we go? thou hast the words of eternal life" (John 6:68).

Watch the Story Come to Life

"Parable of the Sower" video

https://www.lds.org
/media-library/video
/2014-01-029-parable
-of-the-sower?lang=eng

"The Good Samaritan" video

https://www.lds.org
/media-library/video
/1998-05-01-the-good
-samaritan?lang=eng

Learn through Song

"The Wise Man and the Foolish Man," *Children's Songbook*, 281

"On a Golden Springtime," *Children's Songbook*, 88

"Tell Me the Stories of Jesus," *Children's Songbook*, 57

HOW DO PARABLES REMIND US OF JESUS?

After cleansing the temple, Christ taught several parables. Knowing He would soon be leaving the people, He wanted to help them understand and appreciate His gospel so they could stay strong after He was gone.

There is an old saying: "Tell me, I forget. Show me, I remember. Involve me, I understand." Sometimes when we only hear a talk or lesson, it is easy to forget what we have learned. Jesus was the Master Teacher. He often went beyond simply telling people what they needed to learn and instead showed and involved them by using parables, such as those of the good Samaritan and the prodigal son. These stories not only demonstrated the principles He wanted people to remember; they also invited His learners to become involved because they had to take responsibility and figure out how the divine truths in these stories applied to their own lives.

Have you ever looked at a picture with hidden objects in it? At first you see only an obvious image. However, the more you study it, the more you begin to find additional pictures you didn't notice before. Parables are like that. At first you hear a nice story, but the more you think about the story, the deeper meaning you find. Some of the people or items in the story are symbols that stand for something else. A flag is just a piece of cloth, but it is a symbol of a country. A four-leaf clover is just a plant, but it symbolizes good luck. There are many symbols of Jesus. He is the Good Shepherd and the Lamb of God. He is the Light of the World. He is Living Water and the Bread of Life. In many of His parables, the Savior taught about gifts that Heavenly Father offers us freely. When we hear Christ's parables, we can remember Jesus and learn the truths He taught.

Here are some ideas to help you celebrate and learn. Choose what works best for your family!

Parable Charades

As preparation for the game, read the parables together as a family so that children are familiar with them. Write the names of the parables on separate slips of paper and place them in a bowl. Have one family member draw a strip and act out the parable without speaking. The other family members guess which story is being acted out. You can also switch the game around by having the whole family except one person acting out the parable together while the one remaining family member guesses. Here is a list of parables to get you started:

Matthew 13: Sower, wheat and tares, mustard seed, leaven, treasure hidden in the field, pearl of great price, net cast into sea

Matthew 20: Laborers in vineyard

Matthew 21: Two sons and the wicked husbandman

Matthew 22: The marriage of the king's son

Matthew 24: The fig tree

Matthew 25: The ten virgins, talents, sheep and goats

Mark 12: Widow's mite

Luke 10: Good Samaritan

Luke 14: Great supper

Luke 15: Lost sheep, piece of silver, prodigal son.

Luke 16: Unjust steward, rich man and Lazarus

Luke 18: Unjust judge, the Pharisee and publican

Luke 19: The ten pounds

Hidden Talents

Make a list of talents that may or may not be obvious to others. For example, learning a Primary song and singing it or playing it on a musical instrument, making up a dance and performing it, making a treat, memorizing a poem or scripture, showing kindness by giving hugs, and so on. Gather the family and read the parable of the talents (see Matthew 25:14–30). Explain that in Jesus' day, a talent was a large sum of money, but in the parable it was a symbol of anything of great value in our lives such as our testimonies of the gospel or the gifts and abilities we have been given. Let each family member choose a talent from the list, and give a time limit for each member to "develop" his or her talent. Then come back together ready to share with the group.

Hidden Objects

Create a hidden-object shaker. Fill a see-through jar or bottle halfway with sugar or rice. Then place items related to parables inside (a coin, a bean seed, a fake pearl, etc.) and close the lid tightly. Take turns shaking the bottle, uncovering the hidden objects, and trying to identify the parable or symbol they represent.

Wise Steward Game

Fill a bowl with small candies (such as M&M's or Skittles), and give a straw to each family member. Explain that the bowl will be passed from person to person, and whoever has the bowl must use the straw to take as many candies out of the bowl as possible in thirty seconds. To move the candies, players must suck on one end of their straw and place the other end on a candy. If they are sucking hard enough, they can lift the candy out of the bowl and set it aside.

Each family member will most likely end up with a different amount of candy. Some will have a lot, and some will only have a few pieces. Ask each family member to donate whatever portion he or she thinks is fair to the person sitting next to him or her. After all have made their donations, give each person back twice as much as whatever he or she donated. Discuss the parable of the wise steward (see Luke 12:42–48). If a child has only a little candy but gives away much, you could have another discussion about the widow's mite (see Mark 12:41–44).

Service Basket

After reading the parable of the good Samaritan (see Luke 10:30–37), serve people in need by taking them an Easter basket filled with items tied to scripture themes. Here are a few examples, but feel free to think of your own!

Candle: "Let your light so shine before men, that they may see your good works, and glorify your Father which is in heaven." Matthew 5:16

Treat or drink: "Blessed are they which do hunger and thirst after righteousness: for they shall be filled." Matthew 5:6

Music: "For my soul delighteth in the song of the heart; yea, the song of the righteous is a prayer unto me, and it shall be answered with a blessing upon their heads." Doctrine and Covenants 25:12

Soap: "He that hath clean hands, and a pure heart . . . shall receive the blessing from the Lord, and righteousness from the God of his salvation." Psalm 24:4–5

Bath salts or sea salt: "Ye are the salt of the earth." Matthew 5:13

Slippers: "And your feet shod with the preparation of the gospel of peace." Ephesians 6:15

Hair accessory: "But even the very hairs of your head are all numbered. Fear not therefore: ye are of more value than many sparrows." Luke 12:7

Scarf: "Strength and honor are her clothing; and she shall rejoice in time to come." Proverbs 31:25

Lilies or fresh flowers: "Consider the lilies of the field, how they grow, they toil not, neither do they spin." Matthew 6:28

Art print or picture of Jesus: "He is not here: for he is risen." Matthew 28:6

Betrayal Wednesday
OFFERING AND RECEIVING FORGIVENESS

Luke 22:3–6

Then entered Satan into Judas surnamed Iscariot, being of the number of the twelve. And he went his way, and communed with the chief priests and captains, how he might betray him unto them. And they were glad, and covenanted to give him money. And he promised, and sought opportunity to betray him unto them in the absence of the multitude.

See also Matthew 26:46–50; Mark 14:42–46;
Luke 22:47–53; John 18:2–12.

Art Appreciation

***Judas Betraying Jesus with a Kiss,* by James Tissot.** James Tissot was a French artist born in 1836 who originally painted fashionable watercolors, but then he had a religious awakening. He traveled to the Holy Land so that his paintings of Christ would be realistic.

Memory Scripture

"And they were exceeding sorrowful, and began every one of them to say unto him, Lord, is it I?" (Matthew 26:22).

Watch the Story Come to Life

"The Trials of Jesus" video

https://www.lds.org /media-library/video /2010–11–56-chapter -52-the-trials-of-jesus ?lang=eng

"Forgiveness: My Burden Was Made Light" video

https://www.youtube .com/watch?v=E7zwQ _7q-fU

Learn through Song

"Help Me, Dear Father," *Children's Songbook*, 99

"How Will They Know?" *Children's Songbook*, 182

HOW DOES JUDAS' BETRAYAL REMIND US OF JESUS?

Judas was one of Jesus' Apostles and friends. Jesus trusted Judas, but Judas betrayed Him. This betrayal led to Jesus' unfair arrest and trial. Jesus suffered horrible abuse at the "wicked hands" (Acts 2:23) of leaders, soldiers, and people in the crowd. Some people may read about Christ being betrayed, mocked, and crucified and think Jesus' life was taken from Him. This is not so. Jesus had "life in himself" (John 5:26). He could have chosen to stop His suffering and death at any time. Instead, He chose to let it happen, because He knew this was the only way He could save the world. That's how much He loves us. Jesus did not die *because* of Judas, but *for* Judas; not *because* of Pilate and his soldiers, but *for* them. From the cross, Jesus said, "Father, forgive them; for they know not what they do" (Luke 23:34).

We will never have to endure all the suffering that the Savior did, but some friends may choose to turn away from us and some people may treat us unkindly. We can remember Jesus' example and be forgiving. Forgiveness doesn't mean we let dangerous people hurt us over and over. It means we let go of bitter, angry feelings. Instead of seeking revenge, we pardon others when they hurt us, whether intentionally or innocently. We trust God to judge and help them learn.

Sometimes we hurt others. We must learn to always say we are sorry and seek forgiveness. Because of the Atonement, we can repent and Heavenly Father and Jesus Christ will forgive us. Sin brings suffering and sadness. Forgiveness brings peace and joy. Offering and receiving forgiveness can help us remember Jesus and be more like Him.

Here are some ideas to help you celebrate and learn. Choose what works best for your family!

A Lesson in Salt

Teach children that Roman soldiers got paid with salt because it was valuable for adding flavor to and preserving food. The word *salary* comes from the word *sal*, or *salt*. Make a salt picture. Give each family member a piece of black construction paper, and using white Elmer's glue, have everyone draw a picture of something he or she has learned this week. While the glue is still wet, place each paper on a cookie sheet, sprinkle table salt over the glue, and shake the excess salt onto the cookie sheet to throw away later (you may need to help small children). Then, wet a paintbrush and dip it into the watercolor paint of your choice. Press the brush against the salt, and watch the color spread. Continue until all of the salt is covered in colors. Allow to dry, and display your artwork for all the family to see!

Coded Messages

Write a kind message to someone in a secret code. Teach children to number the alphabet letters 1–26, and then write messages by replacing letters with numbers. Show them how to put a comma between each number and a space between each word so the code can be deciphered by the recipient. Another option is to assign a symbol for each letter. This activity can also serve as a chance to introduce children to the Deseret Alphabet—an early phonetic alphabet that pioneers used. Help children look up information about the Deseret Alphabet online and make a message with that "code." You will need to give the message recipient a key to decipher it.

Collecting Pennies

Jesus was betrayed for thirty pieces of silver (see Matthew 26:14–16), a common price paid for slaves. Although those who paid that amount didn't realize it, that equaled a piece of silver for every year of Jesus' life before He began His ministry. Help children gather pennies that were minted in each of the years of their lives, and glue them to a poster board. You could also make this a more permanent keepsake by mounting the pennies on a wooden plaque. Assist them in writing at least one life event that happened each year and influenced them or helped them prepare for the future. For example:

2005 I was born and blessed. My family moved to Georgia.

2008 I went to Sunbeams and gave my first talk.

2013 I was baptized and confirmed. I got my first set of scriptures and memorized the Articles of Faith.

2014 My brother Sam left on his mission.

2015 Grandma passed away. I miss her. I started babysitting my younger siblings.

Secret Service with a Kiss

In some countries, the Wednesday of Holy Week is referred to as "Spy Wednesday," referencing Judas's plot to betray Jesus. Children can be "secret agents" and plan a secret service project either for each other or for neighbors and friends. Consider  making and delivering hot cross buns, a traditional Easter food.

Explain to children that although Judas betrayed Christ with a kiss, we can use kisses to show love instead. Help them cut out paper hearts, and buy a bag of chocolate candy kisses. Choose somebody to surprise, and spread the hearts and kisses on his or her front porch. Ring the doorbell and run away so that no one will know who did the secret service. You can also write loving messages or quotes on each of the paper hearts.

Hot Cross Buns

5½ cups flour

⅔ cup sugar

1 teaspoon salt

1 teaspoon nutmeg

2 packages (or 2 tablespoons) dry yeast

1 cup milk

½ cup butter

1 egg

1 cup currants (found next to raisins at store—do not use raisins)

1 egg white, slightly beaten

Mix yeast with ½ cup warm water. Set aside until bubbly. In the meantime, combine 1½ cups of flour and all of the sugar, nutmeg, and salt in a mixer. In a microwave-safe bowl, warm the butter and milk. Add to dry ingredients and mix. Add the yeast mixture and mix again. While mixing, add the egg, currants, and flour to make a soft dough. Knead well.

Place dough in a greased bowl and cover with a damp towel. Let it rise until double in bulk (about 1½ hours). Punch dough down and place on floured board. Divide dough into 20 pieces. Roll into balls, and place in two round pie pans (if you use a 9x13-inch pan the middle will not cook). Press the blade of a butter knife down into the dough to create deep crosses in the top of each roll. Cover again and let rise an additional 25 minutes.

Bake at 325 degrees F. for 25 minutes, or until slightly golden on top.

Frosting

1–2 cups powdered sugar

½ block of cream cheese, softened

½ teaspoon vanilla

¼ teaspoon almond extract

1 teaspoon water (if needed)

Combine 1½ cups of the powdered sugar with cream cheese, vanilla, and almond extract. Mix well. Add more powdered sugar or water to achieve the right consistency to drizzle over warm buns.

Last Supper Thursday
THE FIRST SACRAMENT

Luke 22:14–16; 19–20

And when the hour was come, he sat down, and the twelve apostles with him. And he said unto them, With desire I have desired to eat this passover with you before I suffer: for I say unto you, I will not any more eat thereof, until it be fulfilled in the kingdom of God. And he took bread, and gave thanks, and brake it, and gave unto them, saying, This is my body which is given for you: this do in remembrance of me. Likewise also the cup after supper, saying, This cup is the new testament in my blood, which is shed for you

See also Matthew 26:17–20; Mark 14:12–17; 22–25.

Art Appreciation

The Last Supper, **by Carl Bloch.** The Last Supper was not only the last time Christ ate with His Apostles during His mortal life; it was also the time when He introduced the sacred ordinance of the sacrament. Carl Bloch's painting of Jesus with His Apostles shows the reverent nature of that holy event taking place in a humble room.

Memory Scripture

"This do in remembrance of me" (Luke 22:19).

Watch the Story Come to Life

"The Passover" video

 https://www.lds.org
/friend/online-activities
/videos/scripture-stories
/old-testament/17-the
-passover?&lang=eng

"The Last Supper" video

 https://www.lds.org
/media-library/video
/2011-10-013-the-last
-supper?lang=eng

Learn through Song

"The Sacrament," *Children's Songbook*, 72

"Before I Take the Sacrament," *Children's Songbook*, 73

HOW DOES THE LAST SUPPER REMIND US OF JESUS?

On the evening before He was crucified, Jesus and His Apostles gathered to eat a meal together. This has come to be known as the Last Supper, but at the time they were actually commemorating the Jewish holiday known as the Passover. Passover was a time to remember when God softened the heart of the Pharaoh and convinced him to free the Israelite slaves. The Lord sent many plagues to Egypt, and finally Moses told Pharaoh that the firstborn son of every family would die because the Israelites were not allowed to go free (see Exodus 7–11). The only ones whose families would be unharmed would be those with faith enough to follow God's command to sacrifice a lamb and mark their doorways with the blood. Death would then pass over that house (see Exodus 12:23). This plague pointed toward the future sacrifice of God's firstborn son, Jesus. He is called the Lamb of God, and through His atoning blood, we can be resurrected and escape death.

When Jesus and His disciples celebrated the Passover together that Thursday night, the Savior instituted the sacrament. He taught that broken bread, like the body of the lamb, would remind them of His body. Wine or water, like blood on the doorways, would remind them of His blood. In 1 Corinthians 5:7 we read that Jesus became "our passover" when He died, delivering us from the bondage of death and sin.

Later that night, the Savior went to the Garden of Gethsemane to begin the Atonement. The garden was a grove of olive trees where people would harvest olives and then crush them with huge weights to obtain the oil. In that garden, Christ took upon Himself the weight of all our sins and sorrows until He bled from every pore. Partaking of the sacrament each Sunday will help us remember Jesus and take His name upon us.

Here are some ideas to help you celebrate and learn. Choose what works best for your family!

Homemade Mezuzah

Jewish people sometimes put a mezuzah on their doors. A mezuzah contains a special scroll of scriptures that are meaningful. Have family members make a scroll of favorite scriptures and place them in a homemade mezuzah. This can be done by decorating a small box or creating a small container using construction paper. Make

sure that the scroll of scriptures fits inside, and hang the mezuzahs by the doorway of each person's bedroom. They can help remind family members to read the scriptures.

Elijah Has Come

Sing the song "If with All Your Hearts" (*Children's Songbook,* 15). Explain that these lyrics are set to a piece of music called "Elijah," by Felix Mendelssohn. He lived around the same time as Joseph Smith and wrote this particular song in 1836. Remarkably, this date coincides with the appearance of Elijah to Joseph Smith and Oliver Cowdery on April 3, 1836, in the Kirtland Temple.

Explain that when Jewish people celebrate Passover, they traditionally leave an extra chair and place setting for the prophet Elijah, in hopes that the prophecy of his coming will be fulfilled (see Malachi 4:5–6). Latter-day Saints know that he has already come. During your Passover dinner or evening meal, encourage children to set an extra place setting with an extra chair as Jewish people do. During dinner, discuss the significance of the sealing power that Elijah restored, which allows us to enjoy forever families.

Olive Fingers

Olives are a typical food in the Holy Land and can remind us of the Garden of Gethsemane, an olive grove. Put a pitted olive on the end of each child's ten fingers. As the child takes the olives off (and eats them if desired), he or she can list ten blessings or ten people who have been good examples.

Destroying Angels Game

Today there is not a destroying angel at our doors, but there are destructive influences that can destroy our families, such as selfishness, criticism, pornography, bullying, too much technology, etc. These things may not destroy us physically, but they can hurt us and others emotionally and spiritually. Sit in a circle and take turns rolling a pair of dice. Every time doubles or the number seven are rolled, the person who rolled it has to say a way that we can protect, avoid, or safeguard ourselves from these "destroying angels." For example:

Don't tease.
Don't say something mean and think it's okay if you quickly say, "Just kidding."
Limit time on the computer or tablet.
Share toys.
Compliment others.
Come when you are called.
Eat meals together.

Passover Seder Meal

Food can provide a powerful, lasting reminder of important principles. Have a traditional meal, or create a drawing on a paper plate of the various foods and discuss their symbolic meaning.

Matzo: The bread of slavery and of freedom.

Lamb shank bone: Represents sacrifice; bone reminds us of God's strong hand and outstretched arm.

Hard-boiled egg: A symbol of spring and new life. As eggs get harder when they cook, so did the Jewish people become stronger through adversity.

Fresh greens (parsley or celery): Represents new life and is dipped in salt water, which represents tears mourning those who drowned in the Red Sea.

Bitter herbs (horseradish): Representing what the slaves had to endure.

Charoses/haroset (chopped apples, nuts, with cinnamon): Like the mortar used to build while in bondage.

Grape juice (in place of wine): Sweetness represents the promise of a better life.

Unleavened Bread

3 cups flour
¼ teaspoon salt
Water

Preheat oven to 400 degrees F.

Combine salt and flour in a bowl. Add water until the dough pulls away from the sides. Add more flour if dough is too tacky.

Turn out onto a floured surface, and use a rolling pin to flatten.

Cut dough into triangles and place on a lightly greased cookie sheet.

Prick dough with a fork several times without puncturing all the way through.

Bake immediately until browned (about 10 minutes), and serve warm or cold.

Good Friday

JESUS' SACRIFICE

Luke 23:33–38

And when they were come to the place, which is called Calvary, there they crucified him, and the malefactors, one on the right hand, and the other on the left. Then said Jesus, Father, forgive them; for they know not what they do. And they parted his raiment, and cast lots. And the people stood beholding. And the rulers also with them derided him, saying, He saved others; let him save himself, if he be Christ, the chosen of God. And the soldiers also mocked him, coming to him, and offering him vinegar, And saying, If thou be the king of the Jews, save thyself. And a superscription also was written over him in letters of Greek, and Latin, and Hebrew, THIS IS THE KING OF THE JEWS.

See also Matthew 27, Mark 15, John 19.

Art Appreciation

Grey Day Golgotha, **by J. Kirk Richards.** An American artist and member of the Church, J. Kirk Richards is admired for his spiritual artwork. His emotional painting style helps us feel what people must have felt when they were with Christ.

Memory Scripture

"Not my will, but thine, be done" (Luke 22:42).

Watch the Story Come to Life

"To This End Was I Born" video

https://www.lds.org
/media-library/video
/2014-01-007-to-this
-end-was-i-born?lang
=eng

"Jesus Is Scourged and Crucified" video

https://www.lds.org
/media-library/video
/2011-10-019-jesus-is
-scourged-and-crucified
?lang=eng

Learn through Song

"To Think about Jesus," *Children's Songbook*, 71

"He Died That We Might Live Again," *Children's Songbook*, 65

HOW DOES GOOD FRIDAY REMIND US OF JESUS?

Jesus was crucified on a Friday, so how can such a sad day be called "good"? The word *good* in English can mean holy, and we celebrate Good Friday because everything good and holy that we enjoy or hope to enjoy comes to us because of Christ's sacrifice. The word *gospel* comes from two old English words—*god*, meaning good, and *spell*, meaning story or news. The gospel is good news, and Christ's Atonement is the core of that good news! Jesus was willing to come to earth. He lived a perfect life. He was willing to suffer and die for us. He was resurrected.

Because of the Atonement of Jesus Christ, we will also be resurrected and we have the opportunity to repent of our sins. We can receive His divine help to lift us during all our trials and sorrows. Because of Christ's Atonement, we can live with God, family, and loved ones again and reach our eternal potential. Because Jesus is good, we can also become good. He chose to become like us so that we can choose to become like Him. That's why we celebrate Good Friday.

Some people like to celebrate Christmas more than Easter because they would rather focus on Jesus' birth than His death. We need to remember that the reason Jesus was born was to fulfill the Atonement. When the wise men came to give gifts to the child Jesus, they presented Him with gold, frankincense, and myrrh (see Matthew 2:11). They gave him gold, a valuable treasure, because Jesus was the King of Kings; frankincense, an ingredient in the incense used in the temple, because Jesus was holy; and myrrh, used anciently to anoint the dead, because Jesus came to die for us. From the day of His birth, Jesus was preparing to die on the cross. His death was necessary to bring about the glad tidings of great joy that began at His birth. Both Christmas and Easter can help us remember Jesus and the joy He brings to all.

Here are some ideas to help you celebrate and learn. Choose what works best for your family!

Crown of Thorns

Make a crown of thorns by braiding play dough into a crown and inserting toothpicks to represent the thorns. Each time a family member makes a sacrifice or performs a small act of service without being asked, he or she will get to pull a toothpick out of the crown as a visual reminder of the gratitude we should feel for Christ's suffering. The goal is to remove all of the "thorns" by Easter.

Jesus' Helpers

Remind children of those who helped Jesus on His last and greatest mission. For example, the Apostles stayed with Him at the Garden of Gethsemane, an angel came to help Him, Simon of Cyrene carried His cross, Joseph of Arimethaea sought permission to bury Him in a tomb, and John promised to care for His mother. Discuss how we can be Jesus' helpers by serving others (see Mosiah 2:17). Invite each family member to write down examples of good people who have helped your family when you were in need. Share what you wrote down, and then encourage children to think of someone who may need their help. Make plans for how your family can serve the people you think of.

Symbols of Christ's Death

Find pictures of items that represent the events surrounding Jesus' death (you can find them in a book, online, or make your own). Discuss what each one represents and how it relates to Christ's trial and Crucifixion. Here are some examples of items:

column	nails	death cloth
garment and dice	lance to pierce His side	the superscription
sponge of vinegar	crown of thorns	
whips	cross	

If you want to see all of the symbols in one place, you can look up images of and information about a bridge leading to Castel St. Angelo in Rome, Italy. It has ten angels sculpted by Gian Lorenzo Bernini. Each angel holds a symbolic reminder of the Crucifixion. Another beautiful sculpture depicting Jesus' death and His mother's grief is *La Pietà,* by Michelangelo. Sculpture and art can be powerful tools for helping us feel and remember important events. After looking at these images and sculptures, discuss how the symbols of Christ's death can help us appreciate the Atonement.

Light in the Darkness

Mark 15:33 says there was darkness over the whole land when Jesus was crucified. There were three hours of darkness in the Old World, and three days of darkness in the

New World (see Matthew 27:45; 3 Nephi 8:20–23). Turn out the lights in your home, and let children experience a room in darkness. Sing "Behold the Great Redeemer Die" (*Hymns*, no. 191) by Eliza R. Snow. Verse five is especially applicable:

He died, and at the awful sight
The sun in shame withdrew its light!
Earth trembled, and all nature sighed,
In dread response, "A God has died!"

Then use a flashlight or light a candle to demonstrate our need for the light of Christ. Read Mosiah 16:9 and other scriptures about Jesus being the light of the world (see D&C 39:2; D&C 93:9; John 1:5; John 9:5). You could reflect on the shock that Jesus' disciples must have felt at His death and how they would have felt like they were in darkness. Then discuss the faithful women who approached Jesus' tomb and how Jesus' Resurrection brought light back to them.

Paper Plate Calvary

Make paper plate models of Calvary. Cut out a half circle in the center of your plate, and fold the flap up to make a hill. Then have children color rocks and grass on the hill. Cut out three brown paper crosses to staple or tape on top, and draw a tomb at the bottom. Display your models somewhere you can see and remember Jesus' Crucifixion.

Fish Symbol

The fish was an early Christian symbol. Perhaps this was because Jesus called fishermen as disciples. Maybe it reminded people that He fed the five thousand with two fishes and five loaves (see Luke 9:13). It could also have been because the Greek word for fish is *ichthys*, which became an acrostic: *Iesous Christos Theou Yios Soter* (Jesus Christ, Son of God, Savior). Because the fish was such a common symbol, early members of the Church of Jesus Christ could mark tombs and meeting places without drawing unwanted attention and persecution. The symbol of a fish became a way to distinguish between friend and enemy. For these reasons, fish is typically served on Good Friday.

Honey Fish

Tilapia fillets, one for each person

Italian-style or seasoned bread crumbs, enough to bread fish on both sides

Parmesan cheese, to taste (about ½ cup)

1 teaspoon powdered ginger

1 teaspoon powdered garlic

1 teaspoon sea salt

Butter

Honey

Thaw fish fillets if frozen.

Pour a generous amount of Italian-style bread crumbs into a glass pan or bowl. Add Parmesan cheese, ginger, garlic, and salt, and stir together.

Melt 1 tablespoon butter in a frying pan over medium heat.

Dip each fish fillet in bread crumb mixture on both sides. Fish should be naturally wet enough to hold crumbs, but coat with egg if needed.

Pan fry fish until cooked through (about 2 minutes per side).

Just prior to removing fish to serving plate, drizzle with a small amount of honey.

Squeeze fresh lemon juice on top, and serve with favorite side dishes.

Salvation Saturday
CHRIST IN THE SPIRIT WORLD

D&C 138:12, 15–16

And there were gathered together in one place an innumerable company of the spirits of the just, who had been faithful in the testimony of Jesus while they lived in mortality; I beheld that they were filled with joy and gladness, and were rejoicing together because the day of their deliverance was at hand. They were assembled awaiting the advent of the Son of God into the spirit world, to declare their redemption from the bands of death.

Art Appreciation

Jesus Teaching in the Spirit World, **by Robert T. Barrett.** Robert T. Barrett is an American painter, illustrator, and member of the Church. He started his career illustrating the scriptures for children and is currently a professor of illustration at Brigham Young University. He uses his talents to bring the scriptures to life for others.

Memory Scripture

"For Christ. . . . went and preached unto the spirits in prison" (1 Peter 3:18–19).

Watch the Story Come to Life

"Gathering of Israel" video

https://www.lds.org
/media-library/video
/2011-03-101-gathering
-of-israel?lang=eng

"Mormon Missionaries:
An Introduction" video

https://www.youtube
.com/watch?v=YGnpH
LS81lY

Learn through Song:

"The Church of Jesus Christ,"
Children's Songbook, 77

"I Want to Be a Missionary Now,"
Children's Songbook, 168

HOW DOES MISSIONARY WORK
REMIND US OF JESUS?

According to the Joseph Smith Translation of the Bible, Jesus' final words during mortality were, "Father, it is finished, thy will is done" (JST Matthew 27:54). His physical body then died, but His spirit body continued to live—as will each of ours after we die. While His body was in the tomb, His spirit went to the spirit world, as described in Doctrine and Covenants 138. He passed through the veil into a different kind of existence that is found right here on this earth.

Some people think Jesus' spirit entered immediately into the physical presence of His Father in Heaven. However, Christ would soon tell Mary Magdalene that He had "not yet ascended to [His] Father" (John 20:17). Instead, Jesus was "received into a state of happiness, which is called paradise, a state of rest, a state of peace" (Alma 40:12).

In paradise He was greeted by a large multitude who had been waiting for Him. He was welcomed by Adam and Eve and all of greatest and most righteous spirits who had ever been on this earth. These spirits had been separated from their bodies for a long time and were anxiously awaiting the Resurrection that was close at hand (see D&C 138:50).

Along with righteous spirits, there were many others who had never known of Jesus while they lived on earth. They had never heard His gospel and had not been baptized. Rather than teaching them directly, Jesus delegated authority and organized the faithful spirits in paradise to visit and teach the unbaptized. He called them to be missionaries. He commissioned them to carry the light of the gospel to all who were in darkness (see D&C 138:29–30). Some would accept the message, and some would not. Either way, Jesus gave every soul the opportunity to learn faith, repent, accept covenants, and progress. As we teach the first principles and ordinances of the gospel, we can be missionaries to help people remember Jesus and be reunited with Him.

Here are some ideas to help you celebrate and learn. Choose what works best for your family!

Five-Finger Prayers

One thing missionaries do is to teach people to pray. Help children learn and teach others the steps of prayer by using five fingers:

(1) Heavenly Father,
(2) We thank Thee for . . .
(3) We ask Thee for . . .
(4) In the name of Jesus Christ,
(5) Amen.

Consider giving children the opportunity to teach this lesson to others multiple times to help them remember it themselves. Grand-parents, home teaching families, visiting teaching sisters, and cousins are usually willing learners!

Indexing and Family Tree

Read John 16:20: "That ye shall weep and lament, but the world shall rejoice: and ye shall be sorrowful, but your sorrow shall be turned into joy." Explain that Christ's death brought grief to His disciples on earth but joy to those in the spirit world (see D&C 138) Talk about baptisms for the dead and why the ordinances performed in temples can help those who never had the chance to hear the gospel. Teach older children how to do indexing and set up online profiles so they can participate in this work. Help younger children create a simple family tree by filling in the names of their parents, grandparents, and great-grandparents. Consider visiting a cemetery and discussing family history work for those who have died. This can be especially meaningful if you live near the burial places of departed family members.

Missionary Egg Hunt

Have an Easter egg hunt using plastic eggs. Fill several eggs with candy, but fill others with instructions to complete a typical missionary activity, such as sewing on a button, ironing a shirt, cooking a simple meal, memorizing a scripture, starting a conversation, bearing a simple testimony, shining shoes, learning to tie a tie, etc. After children find all of the eggs, instruct them to open each one and follow the directions inside. Talk about how missionaries need to be prepared in a variety of ways.

Preach My Gospel Practice

Choose a section from *Preach My Gospel* to use for "companionship study." Divide family members into pairs, and assign each partnership a different section to study. Then come back together and teach each other about what you have learned. Discuss the various aspects of a missionary's duties: study, serve, teach, and find. Have each family member set a goal to improve in one of those areas, and set a date for everyone to report on his or her progress.

Sweet Service

Make sugar cookies and cut the dough into the shape of a missionary necktie, dress, or elder or sister missionary. Decorate and deliver the cookies to neighbors, or share with the missionaries serving near you!

Sugar Cookies

2½ cups flour

¼ cup milk

1 cup sugar

1 egg

½ teaspoon salt

½ teaspoon baking soda

½ teaspoon baking powder

½ teaspoon nutmeg

1 cup shortening

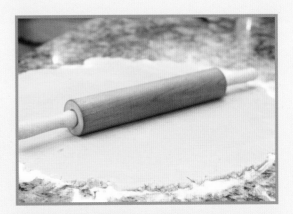

Combine dry ingredients together in a stand mixer or with an electric hand mixer. Add shortening and stir until dough resembles cornmeal.

Combine milk and egg in a liquid measuring cup and whisk together, and then add to dough. Mix until smooth.

Turn out dough onto a lightly floured surface and press or roll out to about ½-inch thickness.

Cut into egg shapes or missionary symbols and place on a lightly greased cooking sheet.

Bake at 350 degrees F. for 10–12 minutes or until lightly browned.

Decorate with frosting and candies.

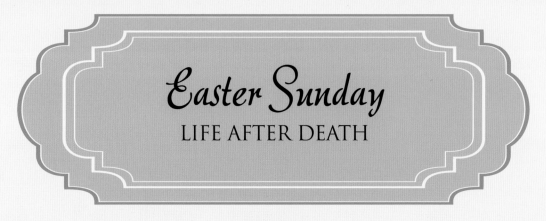

Easter Sunday
LIFE AFTER DEATH

John 20:1–9

The first day of the week cometh Mary Magdalene early, when it was yet dark, unto the sepulchre, and seeth the stone taken away from the sepulchre. Then she runneth, and cometh to Simon Peter, and to the other disciple, whom Jesus loved, and saith unto them, They have taken away the Lord out of the sepulchre, and we know not where they have laid him. Peter therefore went forth, and that other disciple, and came to the sepulchre. So they ran both together: and the other disciple did outrun Peter, and came first to the sepulchre. And he stooping down, and looking in, saw the linen clothes lying; yet went he not in. Then cometh Simon Peter following him, and went into the sepulchre, and seeth the linen clothes lie, and the napkin, that was about his head, not lying with the linen clothes, but wrapped together in a place by itself. Then went in also that other disciple, which came first to the sepulchre, and he saw, and believed. For as yet they knew not the scripture, that he must rise again from the dead.

See also John 20:10–21; 21; Luke 24:13–35; Mosiah 3.

Art Appreciation

Touch Me Not, **by Minerva Teichert.** Minerva Bernetta Kohlhepp Teichert was an American LDS artist who created over four hundred large paintings, many of which showed Book of Mormon stories or temple themes. Her style shares the gentle and warm nature of Jesus Christ by giving impressions of what He must have been like rather than clear images that look like photographs.

Memory Scripture

"The Lord is risen" (Luke 24:34).

Watch the Story Come to Life

"He Lives: Testimonies of Jesus Christ" video

 https://www.lds.org
/media-library/video
/2010–03–07-he-lives
-testimonies-of-jesus
-christ?category=topics
/easter&lang=eng

"Jesus Is Risen" video

 https://www.lds.org
/media-library/video
/2010–11–58-chapter
-54-jesus-is-risen?
category=topics/easter
&lang=eng

"Jesus Is Resurrected" video

 https://www.lds.org
/media-library/video
/2011–10–021-jesus
-is-resurrected?category
=topics/easter&lang=eng

Learn through Song

"Did Jesus Really Live Again?" *Children's Songbook*, 64

"Jesus Has Risen," *Children's Songbook*, 70

"Beautiful Savior," *Children's Songbook*, 62

HOW DO COLORED EGGS
REMIND US OF JESUS?

Eggs have long been a symbol of Easter because they represent new life—the new life that Jesus provided through His Atonement and Resurrection. Because Jesus died and came back to life, we will also be resurrected. Because Jesus suffered for our sins, we can repent and be forgiven. But at Easter time, why do we color eggs? This practice teaches that Jesus offers us not only new life (symbolized by the egg), but He offers to make our lives better (symbolized by the color and decorations).

We call Jesus our Savior and Redeemer, but those words don't necessarily mean the same thing. We call Jesus our *Savior* because He saved us from death and sin. We call Him *Redeemer* because He can change us and help us be better.

At Easter, children love to hide the colored eggs and then find them. This also reminds us that we must seek God and Jesus in our lives. If we lose something very important, we must be willing to put aside everything else and search diligently for it. We know that we will be much happier when we find that item.

People who are missing God and Jesus in their lives must be willing to seek Them. People who don't know the gospel will be blessed by putting aside everything else and searching diligently for the better life the gospel offers. People are happier when they find God and Christ and follow Their teachings. We find eggs by looking in hiding places. We seek God through regular prayer, scripture study, and going to church. When we have found God, we have found what matters most.

Easter eggs are more than just a fun tradition. Coloring and finding eggs can help us remember Jesus and be reminded to always seek Him.

Here are some ideas to help you celebrate and learn. Choose what works best for your family!

Golden Egg Hunt

Have a traditional Easter egg hunt with one addition: an egg that has been hollowed out (if it is a real egg) or left empty (if it is a plastic egg). Paint this egg gold, and teach children that this egg represents Jesus' empty tomb, which provided a golden future for all of us. To further reinforce the idea of an empty tomb, have children help make empty tomb rolls at the end of the hunt (see Matthew 28:6).

Empty Tomb Rolls

1 package frozen roll dough, thawed, or 1 package of crescent rolls, or a favorite homemade roll dough recipe

1 bag large marshmallows (fresh works best)

Cinnamon/sugar mixture (optional)

Press each roll-sized portion of dough into a flat circle.

Sprinkle a small amount of cinnamon/sugar mixture over dough.

Place 1 large marshmallow in the center of each circle and then wrap the dough around the marshmallow. Pinch the dough together firmly to seal the marshmallow inside.

Cover with plastic wrap until rolls rise, or keep in refrigerator overnight before

baking. (*Hint:* it works well to bake in muffin tins in case any marshmallow leaks out.)

Bake at 350 degrees F. for about 15 minutes or until golden brown.

Let children help make these rolls so they can see that after the rolls are baked, the marshmallow will have disappeared and the inside will be empty, just like Christ's tomb on Easter Sunday.

Flower Fun

Lily flowers remind us of the Resurrection because the bulbs lay buried under the ground all winter and then bloom in spring. This reminds us that Jesus was in the tomb and then rose three days later. On a piece of white paper, trace a child's hand. Cut out the shape, roll it into a cone, and tape it closed. Bend each finger piece down to create curled flower petals. Use a green pipe cleaner as a stem and a yellow pipe cleaner folded inside to resemble real lilies. Invite children to create a whole bouquet using the entire family's hands.

Witnesses that He Lives

As a family, review some of the witnesses who saw Christ after He rose from the dead:

Mary

The men on the road to Emmaus

Twelve Disciples and Doubting
    Thomas

Peter, James, and John

Book of Mormon account/other sheep

Saul/Paul

Moroni

Joseph Smith and Oliver Cowdery

The eyes of potatoes can be symbols of these eyewitness accounts of the Resurrection, because each eye becomes a plant from which more potatoes grow. Make a potato print by helping children cut three potatoes in half and carve the following letters backwards into the white part of each potato half (one letter per potato piece): E H I L S V. Make sure to carve the letters as their mirror image, as they will be reversed when stamped. Dip the potato in paint or brush the paint onto the letters, and stamp the potatoes onto paper or cloth to spell the message *He Lives.* Help children write their own personal witness that Christ lives on the paper or cloth under the stamped heading. While working on the prints, you could listen to Handel's "Hallelujah Chorus" from the *Messiah,* which was written specifically for Easter and provides some inspiring background music: https://www.youtube.com/watch?v=BBZ7AfZR9xs

Feast on the Word

Have a special meal using your finest dishware, cloth napkins, etc. At each place setting put one or more scripture references on strips of paper. Collect items that represent each scripture, and place them in a basket in the center of the table. Before or after the meal, go around the table and take turns reading the scripture references and

removing the corresponding items from the basket. Your family can think of your own scriptures and items, or use some of these suggestions!

Matthew 26:14–15	silver coin
Matthew 26:39	sacrament cup
Matthew 27:1–2	small piece of string/rope
Matthew 27:24–26	small soap
Matthew 27:28–30	piece of red cloth
Matthew 27:31–32	large nail
Matthew 27: 35–36	pair of dice
Matthew 27:50–51, 54	a spoonful of earth in a small bag
Matthew 27:57–59	piece of linen cloth
Matthew 27:60, 65–66	round rock
Mark 16:1; Matthew 28:2, 5	small tin with perfumed ointment

Conference Sunday
WHEN EASTER COMES DURING GENERAL CONFERENCE

Doctrine and Covenants 1:38

What I the Lord have spoken, I have spoken, and I excuse not myself; and though the heavens and the earth pass away, my word shall not pass away, but shall all be fulfilled, whether by mine own voice or by the voice of my servants, it is the same.

See also Amos 3:7; D&C 20:55; Articles of Faith 1:9.

Art Appreciation

Christus, **by Bertel Thorvaldsen.** The *Christus* is a marble statue by Danish sculptor Bertel Thorvaldsen. The original is displayed at a church in Denmark. Copies can be found in many LDS visitors' centers throughout the world to remind everyone we are Christians. His hands are open, inviting every child of God to come unto Him.

Memory Scripture

"Whether by mine own voice or by the voice of my servants, it is the same" (D&C 1:38).

Watch the Story Come to Life

"His Sacred Name—An Easter Declaration" video

https://www.lds.org/youth/video/his-sacred-name-an-easter-declaration?lang=eng

Learn through Song

"Choose the Right Way," *Children's Songbook*, 160

"Follow the Prophet," *Children's Songbook*, 110

HOW DOES GENERAL CONFERENCE
REMIND US OF JESUS?

In the Book of Mormon we read, "And those who did belong to the church were faithful; yea, all those who were true believers in Christ took upon them, gladly, the name of Christ, or Christians as they were called, because of their belief in Christ" (Alma 46:15). Latter-day Saints are blessed to know that Christ is the Head of the Church today and that He leads it the same way He has always led His people—through living apostles and prophets.

The Bible contains a lot of truth and many of Jesus' teachings, but He did not stop teaching when the Bible ended. "The Bible is not religion; it is a history of those who had religion. The religion of those who live within the covers of the Bible centered in living oracles. . . . Theirs was a religion of prophets and apostles" (Joseph Fielding McConkie, *Here We Stand* [Salt Lake City: Deseret Book, 1995], 41).

We are blessed today to have that same religion that people in the Bible had. We have living prophets and apostles. Long ago, Peter, James, and John made up the First Presidency. Today other men make up the First Presidency, but they have the same priesthood keys, the same sacred callings, and the same special witnesses of the Lord that Peter, James, and John had.

General conference is a wonderful opportunity to learn from Christ's living servants. As we value their testimonies, heed their teachings, and follow their examples, our faith will increase and we can more fully come to understand and love the Lord and His work. At each general conference, living prophets can help us remember Jesus and learn what He wants us to know, do, and become.

Here are some ideas to help you celebrate and learn. Choose what works best for your family!

Conference Tent

In the Book of Mormon, people pitched their tents toward the temple in order to hear the words of the Prophet. In Mosiah 2:6 we read, "And they pitched their tents round about the temple, every man having his tent with the door thereof towards the temple, that thereby they might remain in their tents and hear the words which king Benjamin should speak unto them."

Set up a conference tent inside the house facing the TV or computer screen, and watch conference from the tent. One way to help children pay attention and stay interested is to label paper cups with words that are commonly used by speakers, such as *faith, love, Atonement, family, service,* and so on, and to put small snacks or treats inside each cup. When children hear a word on one of the cups, they get to have a treat from that cup. You could also have children work on puzzles to keep their hands busy while they listen.

Lost Keys

Play the game "Hot or Cold" to guide children to find keys hidden around the room. Explain that cars won't start and doors won't open without a key. In the same way, the keys of the priesthood, which were lost during the Apostasy, had to be restored so the Church could function and prepare the world for Christ's Second Coming. Our current leaders of the Church have keys and authority to guide us.

Conference Songs

The song "The Books in the Book of Mormon," on page 119 of the *Children's Songbook*, teaches the names and order of books in the Book of Mormon. Use the same tune and replace the words with the names of Apostles to help children remember their names. Steven Kapp Perry wrote a song called "At Conference Time," and your family can download the music to it for free using the address below. You can learn both songs to prepare for general conference and to help remind children of its purpose and value in our lives. (https://desbook.co/ConfTime)

Silhouette Picture

Tape a large piece of butcher paper on the wall, and have each family member stand sideways in front of the paper. Shine a light to cast a shadow of the child's profile on the paper, and have another family member trace the shadow. Cut out the silhouette, and have family members draw or write things spoken about during conference that they want to incorporate into their lives. When anything having to do with Easter or the Atonement is mentioned, children can highlight it with a marker or set it apart with a sticker. After conference, children can keep their silhouettes in their rooms to remind them of what they learned and the goals they made.

Original Apostles' Symbols

Learn about the original Apostles of Christ. Do a camera scavenger hunt, in which teams of family members go around the house or neighborhood taking pictures that include symbols for the early Apostles (listed below). Many of the Apostles' symbols reflect traditions about how or where they died. Notice that John's is a snake in a cup, because people believe he was poisoned and yet survived. Some of the symbols reflect the Apostles' acts, such as Matthew's three purses symbolizing that he was a tax collector.

Peter=keys
James=a shell
John=snake in a cup
Andrew=a cross
Philip=cross with two loaves of bread
Bartholomew=three knives

Thomas=a spear
Matthew=three purses
James "the less"=a saw
Jude or Thaddaeus=sailing ship
Simon=fish

Conference Brunch

Have a special brunch between sessions of general conference. Make an egg dish, such as egg soufflé, quiche, omelets, deviled eggs, or another favorite to go along with the Easter egg theme. Our family has a tradition of making eggs Benedict with what we call "Elder Holland-aise Sauce"!

Eggs Benedict

2 poached eggs per person

Baguette or French bread, sliced—drizzle with olive oil, sprinkle with garlic salt, and toast in oven (at 400 degrees F.) until warm and crisp

Cheese of choice—you can melt it on top of bread slices in the oven if you like

Ham or Canadian bacon, cooked

Spinach or avocado slices (optional)

Garnish, such as chives, parsley, or paprika (optional)

Poach eggs slightly on the runny side (you can look up how to poach an egg online if you haven't done this before).

Place the toppings on the bread in the following order: cheese, ham, spinach, egg, and avocado. Top with Elder Holland-asie sauce and desired garnish.

Elder Holland-aise Sauce

4 egg yolks   3 tablespoons lemon juice
½ cup butter, melted   ½ teaspoon salt
½ cup hot water   Dash of cayenne pepper

Bring some water in the bottom of a double boiler to a simmer.

In the top of the double boiler, whisk the egg yolks together.

Slowly add melted butter, and gradually whisk in hot water.

Continue stirring until thick.

Remove pan from heat before adding lemon juice, salt, and cayenne pepper.

Acknowledgments

Special thanks to Joanna Bjerga, Dayna Checketts, Hatsuho Cook, David Dollahite, Claudia Gassin, Lindsay Gassin, Shauna Gibby, Barbara Jensen, Liz Jensen, Tracy Keck, Whitney Laycock, Alicia Moulton, Lisa Roper, Gian Rosborough, Monika Rosborough-Bowman, Kaleigh Spooner, Kim Stoddard, Charlotte Tidwell, Rachael Ward, Tiffany Webster, Amber Wilcox, Brad Wilcox, David Wilcox, Debi Wilcox, Russell Wilcox, Trish Wilcox, Rochelle Wilde, and the team at thesmallseed.com.

About the Author

Wendee Wilcox Rosborough coauthored the picture book *Practicing for Heaven* with her father, Brad Wilcox. The two also collaborated when they spoke together in a general session of BYU Women's Conference in 2007. Wendee graduated from Brigham Young University with a degree in family science, and she and her husband, Gian, are the parents of two sons, Roman and Brenner. She enjoys serving as the nursery leader in her ward, where she has developed many activities in an effort to help children focus on Christ during holiday seasons.